DATE DUE   APR 0 4

OCT 1 1 06			
GAYLORD			PRINTED IN U.S.A.

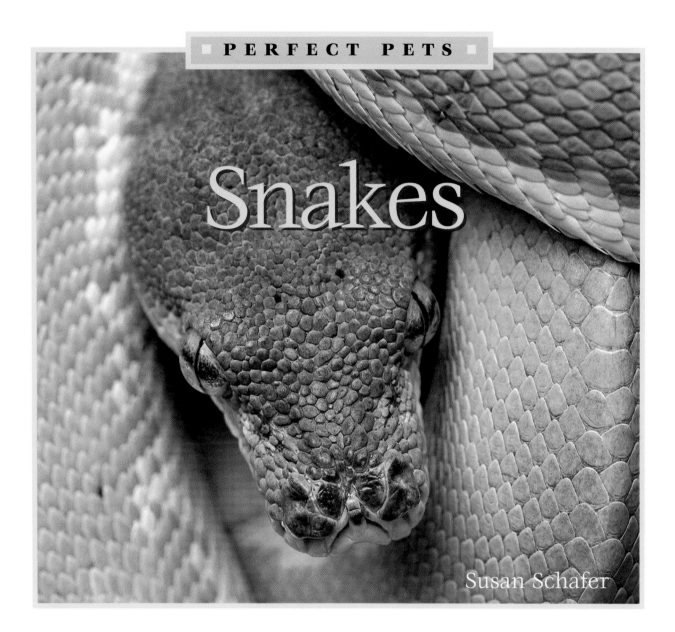

PERFECT PETS

Snakes

Susan Schafer

BENCHMARK BOOKS

MARSHALL CAVENDISH

Benchmark Books
Marshall Cavendish
99 White Plains Road
Tarrytown, New York 10591

Library of Congress Cataloging-in-Publication Data

Schafer, Susan.
Snakes/by Susan Schafer.
p. cm. – (Perfect pets)
Includes bibliographical references and index.
Summary: Presents a variety of information on snakes, including the
physical characteristics and behavior of different kinds, and describes
how to care for a snake as a pet.
ISBN 0-7614-1396-0
1. Snakes as pets—Juvenile literature. 2. Snakes—Juvenile literature.
[1. Snakes as pets. 2. Snakes.] I. Title. II. Series.

SF459.S5 S32 2002   639.3'96—dc21   2001043857

Photo Research by Candlepants Incorporated

Cover Photo: Animals Animals/ Bill Beatty

The photographs in this book are used by permission and through the
courtesy of; Photo Researchers Inc.: Tim Davis, 1; Larry Miller, 3;
National Audubon Society/Robert J. Erwin, 4; Joseph T. Collins, 8; C.K.
Lorenz, 10, 27; Ton McHugh, 13, 20(right); Jany Sauvanet, 14; Karl
Swatik, 16, 21 (top); G. Carleton, 18; E.R. Degginger, 19; John Mitchell,
20(left); S.J. Krasemann, 22; Robert Finken, 24; Cosmo Blank, 26(top);
David T. Roberts, 28; Larry Miller, back cover. Art Resource, NY: Erich
Lessing, 6; Scala, 7. Animals/ Animals: Joe McDonald, 11, 21(low); Carl
Roessler, 12; Paul Freed, 17; C.C. Lockwood, 26(low).

Printed in Hong Kong

6 5 4 3 2 1

To those who believe in the value of snakes.

All snakes have forked tongues.

Snakes

Plug your nose. Now flick your tongue in and out. Can you smell anything? Plug your ears and put your chin on a table. Can you feel anything? You could if you were a snake. Snakes pick up odors with their tongues and sense vibrations through their jaws. They climb without hands, race without feet, and swallow their meals whole. Some snakes, like boas and pythons, can sense heat with their lips!

Snakes have many amazing talents. So why do many people fear them? Some say they are slimy, but they are actually dry and smooth. Some say they are dangerous, but most snakes are harmless and shy. Even the poisonous ones are not dangerous if left alone. Snakes help people by eating mice and rats that destroy crops, get into houses, and spread disease. Still, in many stories throughout history, snakes are the evil villains.

An ancient painting from Egypt shows the sun boat overpowering the giant snake of darkness.

In Egypt, people once believed that every night, the ruler of darkness, a giant snake named Apep, would swallow the sun. In Cambodia, people believed the sun and moon had an evil brother, a snake named Reahou. Reahou lived in the sky and sometimes swallowed the sun or moon, causing an eclipse. The Greeks told stories about a monster named Medusa whose hair was a mass of squirming snakes.

But not everyone hated snakes. The people of Mexico once believed a feathered snake god, Quetzalcoatl, protected their priests and craftsmen. In India, there are stories of a giant snake named Shesha who protects the Earth by coiling around it. Stories from many countries tell of friendly snake gods who turn into rainbows after a storm.

Today people don't fear snakes as much as they used to. After all, snakes have been around for a lot longer than humans have. Our ancestors appeared about 5 million years ago. But snakes—along with their closest relatives, lizards—have been around for about 120 million years!

A Symbol of Healing

The Aesculapian snake from Europe is named after Aesculapius, the Greek god of healing. Two Aesculapian snakes twisted around the staff of Hermes, the Greek messenger god, became the symbol for Greek doctors. Doctors today still use the same symbol.

The wand of Hermes is shown entwined with snakes in a three-hundred-year-old Italian painting.

Milk snakes don't really drink milk, but they will go into milking barns to catch mice.

Snakes

are reptiles. So are lizards, alligators, crocodiles, and turtles. They have scales and are cold-blooded. That doesn't mean their blood is always cold. They just can't make their own body heat like you can. They need the heat of the sun to warm themselves.

Are snakes just lizards without legs? No. Some lizards are legless, and some snakes, such as boas and pythons, have tiny back legs. The legs don't show on the outside except for two little claws, called **spurs**. A male uses the spurs to fight other males and to scratch the female during mating. What sets apart snakes from lizards are shoulders—or rather, their lack of shoulders. All lizards, whether legless or not, have shoulder bones. Snakes do not.

Some California king snakes are born with stripes. Others have bands or rings down their bodies.

Scientists believe snakes lost their legs over millions of years in a process called **evolution**. Without legs, snakes could squeeze into small spaces to find **prey**. Today, there are about three thousand different species of snakes. Some are fat and slow. Others are skinny and fast. They live above ground or underground, in or around water, and in trees.

Wherever they live, most snakes belong to a large group called the **typical snakes**. Many typical snakes make good pets. Rat snakes, gopher snakes, milk snakes, and king snakes are hardy and easy to handle. King snakes, however, eat other snakes, so never keep two together. In fact, most snakes do better if kept alone.

Boas, pythons, wart snakes, thread snakes, and blind snakes are **primitive snakes**. The earliest snake **fossils** looked like pythons. Boas and pythons can get very big. The **reticulated python**, which gets its name from its netlike pattern grows to more than thirty feet (ten meters). A snake that size could stretch across four couches set end to end. Boa constrictors grow to ten feet (three meters). Another boa, the anaconda, is not quite as long as the reticulated python, but can weigh as much as two pro football players.

Toughened folds of skin form a snake's scales.

Unlike fish, sea snakes must occasionally come up for a breath of air.

Cobras, coral snakes, sea snakes, vipers, and pit vipers are poisonous, but some are more dangerous than others. The most poisonous is a sea snake that lives in the ocean off the coast of Australia. It is one hundred times more deadly than any land snake. Never handle a poisonous snake or bring one home. The risk of being bitten is too great, and its venom can cause bodily damage or even death.

If you want a pet snake, make sure it did not come from the wild. Many people now breed snakes in **captivity**. Captive-bred snakes do better than snakes caught in the wild. Contact a **herpetological** society near you to find someone who raises snakes. Ask him or her for information about taking care of one.

A Big Ball of Snakes

Most snakes live alone. But some, such as North American garter snakes, gather in dens during the winter. Thousands den together in the same cave. In the spring, they leave the den, forming big, squirming balls as the males try to mate with the females.

Rattlesnakes crowd together in a winter den.

Just like a vine, a tree snake curls around jungle branches.

Snakes

are masters of disguise. Most are **camouflaged** to blend into the background so they can hide. Tree snakes are brown or green, like branches and leaves. Ground snakes are the colors of dirt, rocks, or fallen leaves. Water snakes are muddy brown or mossy green. When they hold perfectly still, they are hard to see. Some people are afraid of seeing snakes, but snakes don't want to be seen, either. Many animals, including other snakes, eat them.

These young green tree pythons are missing the pigments in their skin that would make them green.

Snakes of a Different Color

Snakes have black, yellow, red, and blue pigments in their skin that give them their color. Albino snakes are missing pigment. Total albinos are missing all four colors and are milky white. Others are part albino. A snake missing blue pigment will look more orange. A snake missing red, blue, and black will look yellow. Albino snakes rarely survive in the wild because it is easy for their predators to see them.

A cobra spreading its "hood" looks much larger than it really is.

Have you ever had someone scare you? Did you jump or run away? If a snake's camouflage doesn't work, it will try to scare its **predator** until it can escape. A cobra stands up and flattens its neck. A rattlesnake rattles its tail. A gopher snake hisses and vibrates its tail like a rattlesnake. A garter snake squirts smelly goo, called musk, at its enemy. A pet garter snake might smear your hand with musk when you pick it up.

A hognose snake fakes its death.

What a Faker!

The hognose snake tricks its predators by pretending to be dead. When frightened, it flips on its back, hangs out its tongue, and holds perfectly still. Many predators, such as cats, lose interest when their prey doesn't wiggle. When the danger passes, the hognose flips back over and goes on its way.

Some snakes are not camouflaged yet can still protect themselves. Coral snakes are decorated with bands of color that are usually red, black, and yellow. Their colors warn predators that they are poisonous. Predators learn to stay away from them. That's good for harmless milk snakes because they look like coral snakes. Predators are tricked into thinking they are dangerous.

Snakes are hunters and can follow prey using their tongues. When a snake sticks out its tongue and waves it in the air, odors cling to it. When the tongue is pulled in, the odors pass through two holes in the roof of its mouth. In this way, a snake can find its next meal, even in the dark.

Boas and pythons don't need eyes or a tongue to see in the dark. They have small pits in their lips that sense the heat given off by prey. They can tell from the "heat picture" if prey is small enough to eat or if a predator is nearby. A pit viper, such as a rattlesnake, has two pits under its nose that do the same thing.

Unlike many other poisonous snakes, a coral snake has tiny fangs.

A Burmese python uses its muscular body to squeeze its prey.

If a rattlesnake loses a fang, a new one will grow in its place.

Snakes hunt without hands. A fast snake, such as a racer snake, chases down its prey and strikes with its mouth. Others, such as king snakes and pythons, **constrict** their prey. They wrap their bodies around their victim until it can no longer breathe. Many snakes use their tongues to sense where their prey lives. Then they sit and wait for it to pass by.

Poisonous snakes use fangs to shoot poison, or **venom**, into their prey. Fangs work like the needles doctors use to give you injections. The venom kills the prey and begins the process of digestion, making it easier to swallow.

Could you swallow a whole turkey or a watermelon in one gulp? No, and you shouldn't try. One reason is that your mouth is not big enough. A second reason is that you would choke. But snakes always swallow their food whole.

They have special joints in their jaws that are like rubber bands. When the joints stretch apart, snakes can swallow food much bigger than their own heads.

Snakes don't have outer ears, but they have inner ones. Sound vibrations pass through the ground, along a snake's jaw, and into the inner ears. Snakes hear people and other big animals coming. They can get out of the way before getting stepped on.

An egg-eating snake stretches its mouth around a chicken egg.

Who's Eating Whom?

Mexican moccasin snakes have short, yellow tails that look like worms. Wiggling their tails, they curl up to wait. When birds, lizards, or frogs come to eat the phony worms, they get eaten by the moccasins instead.

A young cantil—a kind of moccasin—wiggles its bright yellow tail like a worm.

Garter snakes are alert and active.

Keeping

a snake is a big responsibility. It must be checked every day. It needs a supply of fresh food. If it gets sick, you need to take it to a **veterinarian** who treats reptiles. Even choosing a snake is a challenge. It should be eating regularly and have a firm, rounded body. It should not have reddish, irritated skin or gums with cheesy patches, called mouth rot.

Snakes are **carnivores**. Many eat rodents, such as mice or rats. Others eat lizards, snakes, amphibians, fish, birds, insects, and earthworms. Find out what your snake eats before you bring it home.

Garter snakes and ribbon snakes make gentle pets. Giant boas and pythons, however, are not good choices. They can be hard to handle and can cause serious injury. Ball pythons, however, are small enough to keep safely. They grow to about three feet (one meter), a little longer than a baseball bat.

Never leave a live mouse or rat in a snake's cage. It may bite or chew on the snake.

Get a cage ready before you bring your snake home. It can be made of wood, acrylic, fiberglass, or safety glass. Snakes are escape artists, so make sure it has no holes large enough for the snake to pass through, or loose doors. The top and at least two sides should be covered with soft screen for air movement. Sharp screens will injure the snake, and a closed-in cage with no ventilation will act like an oven and kill your pet.

You will need to line the bottom of the cage with a **substrate**. The substrate is the material that your snake will live on top of. It can be potting soil, peat of sphagnum moss, hardwood mulch, paper, indoor/outdoor carpeting, or sawdust. Do not use cedar shavings, which can irritate a snake's skin. Never use gravel, sand, or cat litter, which can kill a snake if it is swallowed.

Snakes need a dark place to hide. Buy a hide box or make one out of plastic, cork bark, or a hollow branch. It should be large enough for your snake to coil up inside. Put the hide box on top of the substrate.

Cobras do not really dance to music. They simply move when the person moves.

Will You Dance With Me?

Snakes like rat snakes, gopher snakes, cobras, and rattlesnakes sometimes fight over females. Pushing and twisting their necks together, one male tries to pin down the other. Sometimes they rear up in the air, looking like dancers at a fancy ball. The winner of the fight will get the female.

A snake usually sheds its skin in one long piece.

All snakes need dry cages, but make sure you give yours a drinking bowl or a water pan. The pan should be large enough for the snake to crawl into but shallow enough for it to get out of. Snakes can drown if trapped in deep water.

A snake sheds its skin every time it grows. To shed its skin, a snake will rub its body against a rough surface. A rock placed in your snake's cage will help it do this. This skin comes off inside out, just like your socks when you pull them off from the top. A snake is ready when its skin turns cloudy or "blue." Some snakes won't eat when they are blue. After they shed, they should begin eating again. If they don't, call your veterinarian.

Giant pythons may seem gentle, especially if they are cold, but they can be dangerous if startled or disturbed.

A Mojave rattlesnake warms up in the sun before going out to hunt.

During the day, your snake will need a "hot spot" at one end of its cage. Use a heat lamp, heating tape, heating pad, or a hot rock. Do not use ultraviolet (UV) or black lights. They can damage your snake's eyes.

Hot spots should be 84° to 86° F (28.9° to 30° C). Your snake will soak up heat until its temperature is just right. If it stays in the heat all the time, that could mean the temperature of the hot spot is not warm enough.

Once a snake warms up, it will move to a cooler area. The cool part of the cage should be 76° to 78° F (24.4° to 25.5° C) day and night. If your snake needs extra heat at night, use a red heat lamp. It can't see red light, so it will think it is dark.

Most snakes eat about once a week. They are hungry when they turn toward you and flick their tongue faster than usual. If yours stops eating and loses weight, call a veterinarian.

Clean the cage every day. Change the substrate every two weeks, or sooner if it gets dirty. A dirty cage can make your snake sick.

Never let pet snakes go in the wild. Pet snakes can't survive on their own. They don't know where to hide or find food. They slowly starve to death.

Snakes do not make good pets for everyone. If you decide you want one, make a commitment to take good care of it. Your snake will reward you with many years of healthy life.

Fun Facts

Snakes can't blink because they don't have eyelids. Instead, they have gogglelike scales that cover their eyes and protect them from getting scratched.

The African egg-eating snake can swallow a chicken egg whole. Breaking the egg in its throat, it gulps down the insides and spits out the shell.

The fastest snake is the African black mamba. Scientists believe it can slither at 10 to 12 miles (16 to 20 kilometers) per hour. The fastest humans sprint at about 25 miles (40 km) per hour.

Two-headed snakes are actually conjoined twins. Although they rarely survive in the wild, they have lived for many years in captivity.

Most snakes have only one lung, which is long and skinny like the snake.

Many snakes, such as boas and rattlesnakes, hold their eggs inside their body until they hatch. The young are then born live.

To glide from tree to tree, Asian flying snakes coil on high branches, dive into the air, and then pull in the muscles on their underside to make themselves into a long parachute.

Most pythons coil around their eggs to keep them warm until they hatch.

Glossary

camouflage: to hide by blending into the background scenery

captivity: being kept in a closed-in area, such as a cage

carnivore: an animal that eats other animals

constrict: to squeeze

evolution: a process of gradual change. In terms of the biology of animals, the process by which animals develop certain characteristics over thousands of years to ensure their survival

fossil: the hardened remains of a plant or animal that lived long ago

herpetological: having to do with reptiles and amphibians

predator: an animal that lives by killing and eating other animals

prey: an animal hunted for food by another animal

primitive snake: a type of snake that has been living on Earth since the earliest times

reticulated python: a large python from Southeast Asia

spurs: small, underdeveloped legs on boas and pythons

substrate: the base on which an animal lives, such as soil

typical snake: any snake other than a boa, python, or blind snake

venom: a poisonous matter secreted by some snakes

veterinarian: a doctor who takes care of animals

Find Out More About Snakes

Books

Markel, Ronald G. and Richard D. Bartlett. *Kingsnakes and Milksnakes: Everything about Purchase, Care, Nutrition, Breeding, Behavior, and Training*. New York: Barron's, 1995.

Mattison, Chris. *The Care of Reptiles and Amphibians in Captivity*. Revised third edition. London: Blandford Press, 1992.

Mattison, Chris. *Keeping and Breeding Snakes*. Fully revised edition. London: Blandford Press, 1998.

Mehrtens, John M. *Living Snakes of the World in Color*. New York: Sterling Publishing Co., 1987.

Websites

Visit *www.sonic.net/melissk/society.html* for a list of herpetological societies, reptile veterinarians, and snake care articles.

Check out *www.thesnake.org* for information on snakes and snake pets.

Index

Page numbers in **boldface** are illustrations.

About the Author

Susan Schafer has studied snakes around the world, from the deserts and forests of North and South America to the islands of the Galapagos, Australia, and New Zealand. She is the author of *Turtles* and *Lizards* in Benchmark Book's Perfect Pets series. She has also written books about lions, tigers, vultures, the Galapagos tortoise, and the Komodo dragon. She lives on a ranch with her husband, dogs, and horses outside San Luis Obispo, California, where she loves to see the gopher snakes and king snakes that share the land.